D1074527

FEB - - 2001

LI

Nature's Fury

TORNADOES

Cari Meister

ABDO
&
Daughters

Visit us at
www.abdopub.com

Published by ABDO Publishing Company, 4940 Viking Drive, Edina, MN 55435.
Copyright ©1999 by Abdo Consulting Group, Inc. International copyrights reserved
in all countries. No part of this book may be reproduced in any form without written
permission from the publisher.

Printed in the United States.

Edited by: Paul Joseph
Art Direction: John Hamilton
Contributing Editor: Morgan Hughes

Cover photo: AP/Wide World Photos
Interior photos: Digital Stock, pages 1, 3, 4-6, 8, 9, 11, 15, 23, 25-28, 30, 31
              AP/Wide World Photos, pages 13, 14, 17, 21
              National Oceanic & Atmospheric Administration, page 22

Sources: Dennis, Jerry. *It's Raining Frogs and Fishes: Four Seasons of Natural
Phenomena and Oddities of the Sky.* New York: HarperCollins Publishers, 1992;
Kahl, Jonathan D.W. *Storm Warning: Tornadoes and Hurricanes.* Minneapolis:
Lerner Publications Company, 1993; Lane, Frank W. *The Violent Earth.* Topsfield,
Massachusetts: Salem House, 1986; Laskin, David. *Braving the Elements: The
Stormy History of American Weather.* New York: Doubleday, 1996; Various articles
on http://www.usatoday.com. WEATHER section.

Library of Congress Cataloging–in–Publication Data

Meister, Cari.
    Tornadoes / Cari Meister
      p. cm. — (Nature's fury)
    Includes bibliographical references and index.
    Summary: Discusses the nature, causes, and dangers of tornadoes, tornadoes of
the past, and ways to survive them.
    ISBN 1-57765-081-6
    1. Tornadoes—Juvenile literature. [1. Tornadoes] I. Title. II. Series: Meister,
Cari. Nature's fury.
QC955.2.M45 1999
551.55 '3—dc21   98-12064
                                                        CIP
                                                        AC

CONTENTS

Tornadoes 4

From Thunderstorm To Tornado 8

Strange, But True 12

Famous Tornadoes 15

Inside A Tornado 18

Waterspouts 20

Predicting Tornadoes 22

Staying Safe 27

Internet Sites 29

Glossary 30

Index 32

TORNADOES

WHEN TORNADOES WHIRL INTO EXISTENCE, HEAD FOR cover! Many people consider tornadoes to be nature's fiercest storms. In just a few seconds, a tornado can blow up a house. In just a few minutes a tornado can flatten an entire neighborhood. Tornadoes weave a path of destruction. They have no respect for anything, including human life.

A tornado is a violent windstorm that spirals around a center of low pressure. Inside a tornado strong winds twist around and around. The winds inside a tornado can get up to 300 miles per hour (483 kph) and can have a lifting force of 100 tons (90.7 metric tons). The winds are so strong and powerful that they create a vacuum. The vacuum sucks up anything that the tornado passes. Tornadoes suck up furniture. Tornadoes suck up animals. Tornadoes even suck up people.

Tornado damage in Saragosa, Texas.

Tornadoes suck up items and then spit them back out later. Sometimes, tornadoes get rid of objects right away. Other times, tornadoes carry objects until the tornado loses power. People often find objects far from where they were collected. A jar of pickles was once found 25 miles (40 km) away from where a tornado snatched it. Strangely, the jar was let down gently. It was not broken.

Humans and animals sucked up into a tornado usually do not survive. Some die from being

A tornado at the end of its lifespan "ropes out" near Cordell, Oklahoma.

bounced around inside the funnel. Some die when the tornado releases them. A tornado's force is so great that when people and animals hit the ground, they usually die instantly.

Because of their shape, tornadoes are also called twisters. Twisters are always cylindrical, but they come in many forms and sizes. Some tornadoes are long and skinny. Others are short and fat. Some people have said that tornadoes look like the heads of anteaters, searching for food on the ground. Other people say that tornadoes look like big black funnels.

Tornadoes can be a few feet across, or as wide as a mile. Some tornadoes last only a few seconds. The longest tornado on record lasted seven hours.

Tornadoes appear in a variety of colors. A pure tornado is white. You usually don't see white tornadoes, though. Tornadoes take on the color of the dirt around them. When a tornado strikes over red dirt, it sucks up the red dirt. This is why the tornado looks red. When a tornado strikes over black dirt, the tornado will appear black.

Tornadoes strike all over the world. The United States, however, is hit more than any other country. About 75 percent of all reported tornadoes occur in the United States. Every state has suffered a tornado at one time or another.

Most tornadoes in the United States occur in Tornado Alley. Tornado Alley runs from North Dakota through Nebraska, Kansas, Missouri, central Oklahoma, all the way to north-central Texas. Usually tornadoes strike in late spring and early summer. The weather conditions are ripe for tornadoes during these times.

About 700 tornadoes touch down in Tornado Alley every year. Approximately 250 more touch down in the United States every year outside of Tornado Alley. Some tornadoes are disastrous, destroying homes, killing animals, people, and trees. However, the vast majority of tornadoes are small, and less forceful.

Tornadoes are very common in Tornado Alley, where cool, dry air from the north and warm, moist air from the Gulf of Mexico collide.

cool dry air

Tornado Alley

warm moist air

Average number of tornadoes per year

9 7 5

(per 10,000 square miles)

FROM THUNDERSTORM TO TORNADO

ALL TORNADOES FORM OUT OF THUNDERSTORMS. However, less than one percent of all thunderstorms produce tornadoes. Let's say it's tornado season in Tornado Alley. A thunderstorm roars in the distance. Heavy rain starts to fall. The radio reports hail the size of golf balls in the next town. Some of the clouds are low to the ground.

You notice that the clouds are not any lower than they were last week. The week before, the clouds only brought two inches (five cm) of rain. They did not bring a tornado. It's still raining outside, but nothing looks or feels unusual. The storm probably won't bring a tornado this time, but keep tuned into the weather station, just in case. Tornadoes sometimes appear without warning.

Lightning strikes in southeastern Arizona.

After a few minutes, you look outside again. It may or may not be raining anymore, but it feels very hot and sticky. There is not much wind. Everything feels very still. When you walk outside, you see big, bulging, pouch-like clouds that seem really low in the sky. Watch out! The pillowy-looking clouds are called mammatus clouds. These are one of the first signs that a thunderstorm might be in the process of creating a tornado.

Mammatus clouds tell us that there are a lot of heavy updrafts and downdrafts near the clouds. If a tornado is going to appear, the next thing that will happen is that the lower part of the thunderstorm cloud will rotate. The rotating portion is a wall cloud. The storm may stop there. On the other hand, part of the wall cloud may drop to the earth in the shape of a funnel. When the funnel touches ground, it's officially a tornado.

The tornado spins faster and faster, picking up dirt and other objects in its path. You hear loud noises. It sounds a little like a freight train. Watch out! Seek shelter! You may only have a few seconds! The noise you hear is the

A wall cloud over
west Texas.

sound of the rocks, sticks, and other debris picked up by the tornado. Inside the tornado, the pieces of debris hit each other so hard and fast that loud noises echo.

Only a severe thunderstorm can produce a tornado. A severe thunderstorm has strong wind shear. A regular thunderstorm does not. If a storm has strong wind shear, it means that the winds blowing on the top part of the storm clouds are more powerful than the winds blowing on the lower part of the clouds. The winds push up against each other. The winds get faster and faster. The cloud spins, forming tighter and tighter circles.

Strong updrafts and downdrafts stretch the already rotating updraft, called a vortex. As the vortex gets thinner (from stretching) it spins faster. During this time, you can't see that a tornado is forming. This is going on inside the clouds. When the vortex drops below the cloud's bottom, it's a funnel cloud. When it touches ground, it's a tornado. If you are worried about a tornado forming, keep tuned to your local TV or radio station.

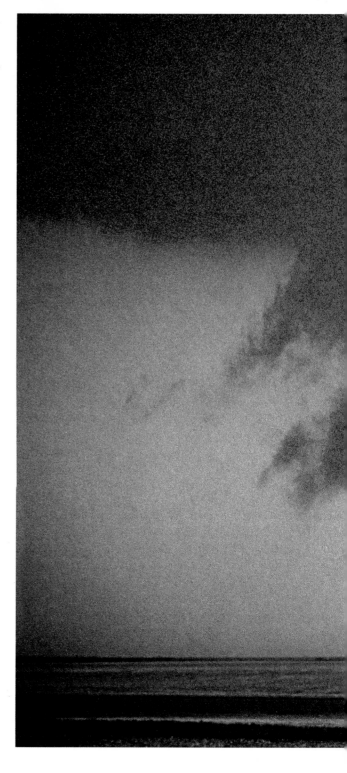

The same west Texas wall
cloud as the previous page.
Now a tornado has descended
from it.

STRANGE, BUT TRUE

TORNADOES ARE DANGEROUS, POWERFUL STORMS. THEY bring ruin to towns all across the world. They smash cars. They flatten homes. They uproot trees. Over the years, people have seen tornadoes do strange things.

People running for shelter in a tornado sometimes find themselves suddenly naked. The suction power of a tornado can pull the clothes right off your body. Several people have told of instances where tornadoes have sucked their shoes right out from under them!

The conductors waiting for trains in Lubbock, Texas, on May 11, 1970, witnessed a strange sight. A tornado pushed a locomotive train (that had its brakes on!) 150 feet (46 m) along the track. The train weighed over 45 tons (40.8 metric tons)!

Tornadoes can cause strange things to happen on a farm. Cows fly through the air. Corn feed gets stuck on barn walls. And perhaps the strangest of all—the depluming of chickens. This means that a chicken's feathers are stripped from its body. After a tornado, farmers often find groups of dead, featherless chickens. Experts do not agree about what causes depluming. Some experts believe that the hollow quills of the feathers expand and explode when chickens are inside a tornado's vacuum. Other experts believe the feathers are somehow blown out of the chicken. One woman in Oklahoma found hundreds of chicken feathers stuck in trees. A tornado had deplumed her chickens. The force was so great that it pushed the chicken feathers deep into trees.

Sometimes tornadoes pick things up in one place and deposit them far away. Everything a tornado sucks up eventually comes down. Just not in the same spot.

An overturned house in Griffen, Indiana, was blown more than 50 feet (15 m) off its foundation on March 21, 1925.

This accounts for the "snake storm" in Memphis, Tennessee, in 1877. One day, baby snakes poured from the sky. People thought it was a curse. Others thought the world was ending. In fact, the baby snakes were sucked out of a nearby pond by a tornado. The tornado released the snakes over the city.

Sometimes tornadoes skip over a particular house, or a person lives through something that seems impossible. In 1984, a tornado picked up a man in Wichita Falls, Texas. The man remembered whirling around inside the tornado. The amazing thing was that he lived. A magazine reported his story:

"During a tornado in Wichita Falls, a man was blown out of his exploding house. Like Dorothy, he glimpsed others in the funnel. A house trailer rotated near him, and in the window he could see the terrified face of one of his neighbors. (She did not survive). Flying ahead of him was a mattress. If I could reach that, he thought, I'd just go to sleep. He then lost consciousness and awoke on the ground, wrapped in barbed wire."

Tornadoes usually do not strike twice in the same place. Scientists believe that a town is likely to be hit by a tornado only once every 250 years. Imagine what it was like for citizens of Codell, Kansas. Tornadoes touched down in Codell on the exact same day for three years in a row!

An aerial view of Xenia, Ohio, which was hit by tornadoes late April 4, 1974, killing 35 persons and injuring many others.

FAMOUS TORNADOES

ON MARCH 18, 1925, THE WORST TORNADO OUTBREAK IN history struck. The storm devastated parts of Missouri, Illinois, and Indiana. It was a huge system—which included eight separate tornadoes—that destroyed everything in its path.

When the storm was over, survivors looked at the land in astonishment. The tornado's path was more than one mile (1.6 km) wide! It claimed 792 lives, and 13,000 people were seriously injured. Another 11,000 people could not return to their homes. The tornado leveled thousands of homes and made thousands of homes unlivable. The tornado of March 18, 1925, lasted for more than 3 hours. Its one mile (1.6 km) wide path of destruction ran a length of 219 miles (352 km).

A deadly F-3 tornado roars across Oklahoma.

Some tornadoes have wiped out entire towns. On May 25, 1955, there were 187 houses standing in the small town of Udal, Kansas. But that night, following a tornado, only one house remained untouched. The tornado completely smashed 170 houses, and 16 were ruined beyond repair. Tragically, 80 people died. Another 270 people were injured.

Time magazine reported on the tornado: "Railroader Fred Dye was snatched out of his shoes, whirled outdoors, and thrown alive up a tree. Barber Henry Norris went to bed, woke up unhurt in the street: 'I don't know how I got there.' Will Sweet and his wife cowered in a back bedroom until it was over, then opened the door and found the rest of the house gone. Norman Lanning huddled with his wife and three children against the kitchen wall by the refrigerator, which skidded away; the wall was the only thing left standing in the area, and it saved them."

On April 3 and 4, 1974, a series of tornadoes ravaged the eastern half of the United States. As many as 148 different tornadoes brought damage to 13 states. The tornadoes sprung up as far south as Mississippi and as far north as New York. More than 300 people died, and more than 6,000 were injured. An estimated 27,500 families suffered losses and roughly $600 million in damage was reported.

A series of tornadoes like this is called a tornado outbreak. A tornado outbreak occurs along a line of thunderstorms. A long line of thunderstorms is called a squall line.

The most amazing tornado story comes from Will Keller— the only person to have ever looked up into a tornado's funnel. On June 22, 1928, a tornado struck his Kansas farm. As the tornado approached, Will raced his family into the storm cellar.

Just as he was about to close the latch, the tornado lifted up off the ground. Will stood there, looking up into the twister. He was mesmerized by what he saw. Will later brought his story to the National Weather Service office. This is what he said:

"I looked up, and to my astonishment I saw right into the heart of the tornado. There was a circular opening in the center of the funnel, about 50 to 100 feet (15 to 30 m) in diameter and extending straight upward for a distance of at least a half a mile (.8 km). . . The walls of this opening were rotating clouds and the whole [tornado] was brilliantly lighted with constant flashes of lightning, which zig-zagged from side to side. . . Around the rim of the great vortex small tornadoes were constantly forming and breaking away. These looked like tails as they writhed their way around the funnel. It was these that made the hissing sound."

Tracy and Sherry Sweet of Charles City, Iowa, hold a photograph of their house after a tornado ripped through the town in 1968. The watch, from her grandmother, and a set of pearls, wedding gifts to each other, were at first lost in the rubble but found later, buried in mud and debris.

INSIDE A TORNADO

Upper-level winds

A tornado is fueled by warm, moist air at ground level updrafting, or flowing upward, at a rapid rate. When strong upper-level and middle-level winds blow in different directions or at different speeds, they help the updraft to rotate. This is called a mesocyclone, or rotating updraft. Winds updrafting this way can reach speeds of 100 miles per hour (161 kph) and heights of 10 miles (16.1 km). When tornadoes form (only half of all mesocyclones produce twisters) they usually appear on the flank, or rear, of the storm.

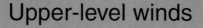

Flanking line of clouds

Mid-level winds

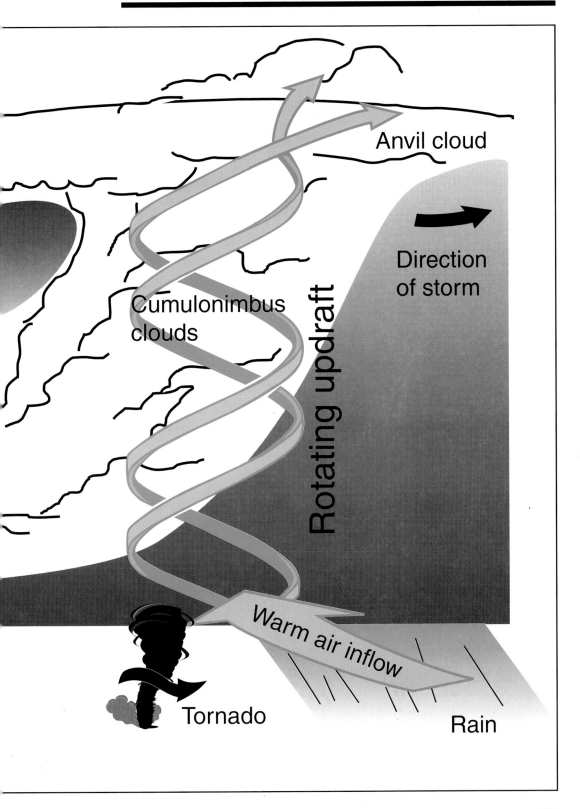

Anvil cloud

Direction of storm

Cumulonimbus clouds

Rotating updraft

Warm air inflow

Tornado

Rain

WATERSPOUTS

WATERSPOUTS ARE TORNADOES THAT OCCUR OVER water. Waterspouts occur over lakes, rivers, and oceans. Like a tornado on land, the bottom part of the waterspout's funnel sucks up things. Instead of dirt and debris, a waterspout sucks up water.

Sometimes waterspouts suck up aquatic animals and deposit them over land. In New York, it once rained tadpoles. In Sweden, it rained worms. In Norway, it even rained rats! Once, a waterspout off Rhode Island picked up fish. A little while later, the fish were pelting people on the streets. Some enterprising citizens collected the fish and sold them!

Waterspouts usually occur from May to September. They usually appear over warm ocean water, near the equator. Waterspouts occur when high layers of cool air meet lower areas of warm air. Off the Florida Keys, almost 100 waterspouts appear every month. People say that waterspouts make hissing and sucking noises.

Like tornadoes, waterspouts can vary in strength. Gentle water-spouts seem barely able to lift water from the ocean. Some water-spouts are very strong. Waterspouts with a powerful vortex can suck up a column of water 20 feet (6.1 m) or more into the air.

Waterspouts can be a few feet wide or they can be hundreds of feet wide. How fast a waterspout can travel varies. Some waterspouts travel as slowly as two miles per hour (3 kph). Other waterspouts travel as fast as 80 miles per hour (129 kph). Inside the waterspout, winds rotate up to 120 miles per hour (193 kph).

Waterspouts do not usually last longer than 15 minutes. Some waterspouts only last seconds. When a waterspout disappears, the water that it sucked up falls back to the ground. The water comes back as rain.

Waterspouts are usually smaller and less destructive than tornadoes. However, waterspouts have been known to kill people. In 1885, near North Africa, five ships were sunk by a waterspout. Another ship, the *Lilian Morris*, reported seeing a 500-foot (152 m) wide waterspout. The waterspout stripped *Lilian's* masts and sails, then threw one crew member overboard.

PREDICTING TORNADOES

IN THE PAST, PEOPLE FOUND OUT ABOUT TORNADOES when they first saw them—usually too late to save their lives. Tornadoes used to kill a lot more people than they do today. Today, there are better ways of warning people that a storm is coming.

The National Weather Service helps people prepare for a tornado by issuing two main warnings. If they issue a tornado watch, they think that a tornado is coming. They don't know for sure. They don't see a tornado yet, but weather conditions are prime. They watch the thunderstorm clouds very carefully.

Once the National Weather Service spots a tornado, they issue a tornado warning. A tornado warning is very serious. Take cover right away!

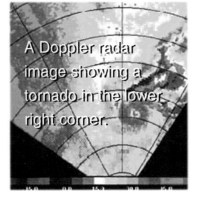

A Doppler radar image showing a tornado in the lower right corner.

Television and radio stations broadcast tornado warnings and watches. Meteorologists usually interrupt regular shows to bring you the latest news. A siren might also go off in your town. Sirens warn people to expect very bad weather.

Scientists are making new weather tools all the time to help meteorologists better predict the weather. Today, meteorologists use satellite and radar systems to track dangerous weather. The most important tool is Doppler radar. Doppler radar is a system that uses radio signals to

A meteorologist at work in a National Weather Service office.

measure wind speed. This is how it works:

1) radar equipment sends out radio signals

2) the radio signals bounce off raindrops and hailstones that are inside clouds

3) the signals return to the radar equipment

4) meteorologists check the returning signals

5) the returning signals help meteorologists track thunderstorms

Meteorologists also use satellites to help predict weather. Satellites circle the earth from space. They carry cameras and other special instruments. The satellites take pictures of clouds from space. The pictures help meteorologists get a better look at storms.

Scientists also send out radiosondes into the sky. Radiosondes look like balloons. They carry special instruments to measure rain, snow, and other weather news. Radiosondes float up high into the atmosphere.

Once a radiosonde is high enough it starts collecting data. Then the radiosonde sends radio signals back to land. The radio signals tell a meteorologist weather information.

We are learning more and more about tornadoes every year. Some scientists try to learn more about tornadoes by getting very close to the deadly storms. These people are called "tornado chasers" because they travel the country chasing tornadoes.

Tornado chasers bring special weather equipment in vans or trucks. They usually spend tornado season in Tornado Alley— where most tornadoes occur.

When a severe thunderstorm produces clouds that look as if a tornado might form, tornado chasers jump into their vans and trucks. Then, they drive towards the tornado!

When the tornado chasers get close, they leave special equipment in the tornado's path. The equipment takes measurements and records storm activity that help us learn more about tornadoes.

Tornado chasing is very dangerous. Never go towards a tornado! Leave tornado chasing to the experts.

A tornado over
west Texas.

A twister roars over
the countryside.

STAYING SAFE

TORNADOES CAN BE DEADLY. THEY KILL PEOPLE EVERY year. You will help your chances of surviving a tornado if you know what to do in an emergency situation.

If you hear that there is a tornado watch, keep alert! Be ready to spring to your shelter. If the tornado watch turns into a tornado warning, seek cover right away. You may have only seconds to save your life.

Before a storm ever hits, you should plan with your family where the best shelter is in your home. Always keep a battery powered radio, blankets, bottled water, and a first aid kit near your shelter.

A wall cloud develops over Texas.

During a tornado, the best place to go is in a storm shelter, or cellar. If you don't have a storm shelter or cellar, go to the basement. If there is not a basement in your house or apartment, go to the lowest floor possible. Find a spot away from windows. Many people survive under stairwells. The more walls you have between you and the outside, the better. When you find your spot, cover yourself up with something big. A mattress is best if there is one available. The least you should do is cover yourself with blankets. That way, if glass and wood speed through the air, you will be less likely to be pierced. Make sure to stay low.

If you are outside when a tornado comes, get inside. If you cannot get inside, find the lowest spot outside. A ditch or the low part of an embankment is best. Lay face down and cover your head with your hands. Do not stand up! Flying debris—like trees, wood, and glass—could kill you instantly.

If you are in a mobile home or car, get out! Tornadoes pick up and destroy mobile homes and cars in seconds. Get to a small building if you can. Large buildings like gymnasiums or supermarkets do not offer as much protection as small buildings. If a wall or roof becomes damaged in a large building, you are more likely to be hit with flying debris.

If you are in school, follow the safety instructions of your teacher. Your teacher will lead your class to the safest place. In most schools, hallways, basements, and stairwells are the safest spots during a tornado. Keep away from windows. Crouch and cover your head.

Tornado damage, Saragosa, Texas.

INTERNET SITES

http://www.usatoday.com

Go to WEATHER. Check out more about tornadoes, thunderstorms, or any kind of weather.

http://cirrus.sprl.umich.edu/wenet/

Check out the weather forecast in your city. Get snapshots of weather through live weather cams.

http://www.nssl.uoknor.edu

The National Severe Storms Laboratory Web site. Go to WEATHER ROOM. Check out tornado intensity charts, and other information about severe thunderstorms.

These sites are subject to change. Go to your favorite search engine and type in "tornadoes" for more sites.

PASS IT ON

Science buffs: educate readers around the country by passing on information you've learned about tornadoes. Share your little-known facts and interesting stories. We want to hear from you!

To get posted on the ABDO Publishing Company Web site, E-mail us at "Science@abdopub.com"

Visit the ABDO Publishing Company Web site at:
www.abdopub.com

GLOSSARY

Cylindrical: Circular, with three dimensions.

Downdraft: A current of air that moves downward.

Mammatus clouds: Bulging, pillow-like clouds that hang down from a storm cloud.

Lightning from a severe storm over southeast Arizona.

Meteorologist: A person who predicts, studies, and measures weather.

National Weather Service: The service that collects weather statistics and issues storm warnings.

Radiosonde: A collection of weather instruments attached to a balloon that is sent off into the atmosphere.

Squall line: A long line of thunderstorms.

Tornado: A violent funnel-shaped windstorm.

Tornado Alley: The area of the United States stretching from the Dakotas to north-central Texas that is prone to tornadoes.

Tornado outbreak: When multiple tornadoes occur.

Tornado warning: The second alert telling people that a tornado has been spotted.

Tornado watch: The first alert telling people that tornadoes may strike.

Updrafts: A current of air that moves upward.

Wind shear: Different wind speed or direction at different altitudes.

A tornado drops from a wall cloud over west Texas. Turn to page 11 to see a photo of the same tornado as it was developing.

INDEX

B
basement   27, 28

C
cellar   16, 27
chickens   12
Codell, Kansas   13
cows   12

D
depluming   12
Doppler radar   22
downdraft   9, 10
Dye, Fred   16

F
Florida Keys   20
freight train   9
funnel   6, 9, 10, 13, 16,
      17, 20

I
Illinois   15
Indiana   15

K
Kansas   6, 13, 15, 16
Keller, Will   16

L
Lanning, Norman   16
Lilian Morris   21
low pressure   4
Lubbock, Texas   12

M
mammatus clouds   8, 9
Memphis, Tennessee   13

meteorologist   22, 23
Mississippi   16
Missouri   6, 15
mobile home   28

N
National Weather
      Service   16, 22
Nebraska   6
New York   16, 20
Norris, Henry   16
North Africa   21
North Dakota   6
Norway   20

O
Oklahoma   6, 12

R
radar   22, 23
radio   8, 10, 22, 23, 27
radiosondes   23
Rhode Island   20

S
satellite   22, 23
school   28
siren   22
snake storm   13
squall line   16
storm shelter   27
suction   12
Sweden   20
Sweet, Will   16

T
Tennessee   13
Texas   6, 12, 13

thunderstorm   8-10, 16,
      22-24
Tornado Alley   6, 8, 24
tornado chasers   24
tornado outbreak   15, 16
tornado warning   22, 27
tornado watch   22, 27

U
Udal, Kansas   15
United States   6, 16
updraft   9, 10

V
vacuum   4, 12
vortex   9, 10, 17, 20

W
wall cloud   9
waterspout   20, 21
Wichita Falls, Texas   13
wind shear   10

32